StrongWords

HEAR ME NOW!

Edited by

Steve Twelvetree

First published in Great Britain in 2004 by
STRONGWORDS
Remus House, Coltsfoot Drive,
Peterborough, PE2 9JX
Telephone (01733) 898101
Fax (01733) 313524

SB ISBN 1 84460 766 6

FOREWORD

Although we are a nation of poetry writers we are accused of not reading poetry and not buying poetry books: after many years of listening to the incessant gripes of poetry publishers, I can only assume that the books they publish, in general, are books that most people do not want to read.

Poetry should not be obscure, introverted, and as cryptic as a crossword puzzle: it is the poet's duty to reach out and embrace the world.

The world owes the poet nothing and we should not be expected to dig and delve into a rambling discourse searching for some inner meaning.

The reason we write poetry (and almost all of us do) is because we want to communicate: an ideal; an idea; or a specific feeling. Poetry is as essential in communication, as a letter; a radio; a telephone, and the main criteria for selecting the poems in this anthology is very simple: they communicate.

CONTENTS

SCION OF HOPE

With my head bowed in sorrow
My mind deeply stirred
I stand, and watch my beloved interred
Soon after the birth of our son

Love nurtures sorrow, sorrow brings pain
Death intervenes, and I still remain.

She is now gone and I am alone
With only my thoughts for a friend
Memories linger, but won't bring her back;
Has my life reached an untimely end?

Then I hold in my arms my newly born son
And realise my grieving is wrong
He is her bequest, through him she lives on
I know that I have to be strong

Judy Berkwicz

SEPTEMBER 11TH - TWO YEARS ON
(Dedicated to all those who have died, on and as a result of 9/11)
(Acts of God)

The days of life they come and pass,
With acts of God through tormented glass
Shattering dreams; humanity's hopes for peace
By breaking news, through a shock release:
As did then on nine-eleven
Four wings they struck with blows from Heaven
They splurged the facts of human terror
To spoil the world with human error;
When burning down to rain below
Where living are, so young will know
Just how keen were those to die
On their cloud in air as they did fly
By smashing, crashing into the sides
In elevation of aeroplane glides
Powered jets so filled with fuel
Bursting into a fiery jewel
Cooking those into disintegration
By the terrorist in occupation.
The disease of mind destroys in frenzy
No sense to make refined amends.
These are people whose god is living
As man outcast with little friends.
And bent the steel and glass did melt
Concrete rubble was soon then dealt
To astound the hearts and souls of people
In a godless manic empty steeple.
So too then did we mourn in pain
The poor then losing as the hate did gain
A rally to break the silent night
Until vengeance reigned by terror's might
To win again the evil crown
Of those menaces,
Who brought the Twin Towers down:

But really is the truth to see
They died through a lack of responsibility
And God fought back as debate demanded
For more human error by those commanded
As man could not lose another war
To find charity for those so poor
To break the values of God's trust
The fight against terrorism,
Became a violent lust;
It cannot find any proportional sense
It's managed without any recompense
For what is lost was a lesson then
When acts of God are the errors of men.
Descript of events in destructive rent
When property dies and lives are spent.
So none now knows where justice ends
Can man rely to God's amends,
Or is there more for us to learn?
How much of life shall in future burn
And shall life's value rise upon
Or shall life's value end in doom when done?
Prayers for hope for those not lost
And prayers for those who've paid the cost
With prices high for desperate men
Can surrender be the true mark of ten?
Where's God's love, for those who died
Or is God's love the Devil's ride?
And love is just a human trait
Upon tenderness distilled from hate
So that man can live amidst his kin
With integrity, friendship and a soul within?

Anthony Rosato

FORGET-ME-NOT

An album of memories, loved faces together,
A vacant chair, never again to hold the dear one,
Tears of sorrow as a mother remembers,
Children who will never know their fathers, mothers.

The terror in the world continues,
Each day more deaths are foretold,
Each day more families lose loved ones,
Will it never cease, a trail that goes cold.

Has mankind stepped away from God
And let the Devil walk abroad?
Have the tragedies brought us closer,
Countries so divided, ideas, opinions, worlds apart?

On the Day of Remembrance we are brought back together,
In the common sorrow of tragedy,
But what happens tomorrow? The world moves on,
The memory dimmed, the families alone.

Let us tell our leaders we want a change,
Go back to basics, standards and values,
Pray to God our Saviour to give us the strength, and
For those tragic souls, whose ghosts whisper *'Forget-me-not!'*

Elizabeth Hiddleston

A Sad Day In America

'Yes' what can anyone say
About what's happened in America today?
Tears and sadness all around
As bombers sent the highest towers to the ground
Too many people hurt and dead all around
Why do we have to suffer in this way?
All we can do is hope and pray
No one deserves what has happened to them today
Now to catch who did it and put them away
This is a very evil, cruel thing that they have done
We will see you in Hell, you have not won
So heartless murdering innocent families
Hospitals are full of casualties
People are desperate to find one another
Asking the whereabouts of their sisters and brothers
Not only did they bomb the highest towers
But they left thousands missing, dead, and America in showers
When we get you, we will put you away
We will make you sorry for what you did this day
People in America, we send you our thoughts and prayers
We in England want you to know that we care
We cannot start to know what you are going through
But believe me, our prayers, our hopes, are all for you
I only wish we could do more
If only to bring some kind of happiness back to your door
Most of all we say a big 'thank you' to those involved
Let's hope we get the evil people and get it solved
Firemen and others, who put their lives at risk
We are all with you to seek out who did this!

God bless America!

Anne Davey

TERRORIST SOLUTION

The headphones are not torturing those men in Camp X-ray.
It's mass indoctrination, they'll be rulers there one day,
Worked well with the Irish problem, 'Freedom fighters all were freed.'
Leaders sit close to the Commons, allowances indeed!

Don't you listen to do-gooders, they usually get it wrong,
With the Fifth Amendment translated, it won't be very long.
These lads will be word perfect when they swear allegiance oath,
For terrorists read Senators, you can be one or both.

Dark glasses help them concentrate as they memorise their lines,
With remote controls inside their mitts to repeat them many times.
Face masks hide their lips, as they learn the words by rote,
Practising their smiles sincere for chasing people's vote.

President Bush has shown the West, the way it must be done,
George W Bush has a lot to learn but they say he's coming on.
Next election in the States, you'll see the whole new cunning plan,
The President in the White House will be pure-bred Taliban.

Think that this is fanciful and I've a screw that's gone amiss?
Anything is possible, ask Adams and McGuinness!

Derek B Hewertson

WAR

So, they want to go to war.
I ask myself why? What for?
We'll lose our loved ones,
our military force.

They'll lose their all -
Women and children,
the old and the sick,
will be caught in the middle.
Blasted into oblivion,
I ask again, what for?

They say, 'Saddam is an evil man.'
Well, are Bush and Blair
to be accountable too?
The responsibility will be
theirs to share.

Do they really think they're immune?
Their consciences will always be there.
No matter what excuses they make,
these innocent lives,
they offer up,
aren't theirs to take.

They will have to atone for their sins,
as indeed, so will bin Laden!

Roberta West

GOD BLESS AMERICA

September 11th 2001
a year never to forget,
when terrorists a battle,
they thought they had won,
into a World Trade Center
thriving at peace
the terrorists flew with murder
in their hearts,
to kill, destroy and maim,
so peace would cease.
But God bless you America
the land of the free,
our prayers and hearts
are with you,
although we're so far away
across the sea.
Our arms are around you
we feel your pain,
we know things will never
again be the same.
But united we stand with
you in a deep bond of love
and our prayers have reached
Heaven we know,
to Jehovah God, our Father
above.

Patricia Gray

SEPTEMBER 11TH

Workers jumping, Twin Towers crumbling
like a stack of dominoes tumbling
viewers gazing in shocked fascination
Two years on echoes still vibrating.

Great nations struggled for domination
amid censure and recrimination.
Were they the wicked aggressors
or benevolent liberators?

Joe Public, weary, turned a blind eye.
Seeing their leaders duck and deny
actions which they failed to justify.
Many shades of truth - what is a lie?

In climate of suspicious doubting
governments are judged and found wanting
people braying for some accounting
amid the scandal daily mounting.

Weep not the dead, enshrined ever young.
Pray for orphans their voices grief-strung
the injured still recuperating
the heroes - their sleep nightmare-ridden.

Man's lack of respect for fellow man
spans time since first creation began.
God have mercy on human frailty
grant us forgiveness in eternity.

Kathleen Potter

SKYQUAKE

My love is like a plane crash
Head-on through the night.
Twisted wires, a smoking pyre
A fire burning bright.
Broken glass is falling,
Rubble fills the sky
And when the dust of my love settles,
Will you ask me why?
My love is like a beacon,
Burning through it all,
A monument to suicide, stupidity and gall.

Alan Gibson

A MESSAGE TO AMERICA

Look at the troubles in restless Ulster
The cries of the bereaved are never quieter
But the folks love jokes and laughter
Without making an awkward stir

Look at the bombs in sunny Spain
Survivors' tears with unbearable pain
But their lives go on not in vain
Without showing any ugly stain

Look at the horrors in the land of the Jews
A road scattered with bloody shoes
But people always, always refuse
To be ruled by the endless tragic blues

Two years after the terrible atrocity
America, you are now facing the reality
You can't escape from evil calamity
So, like we do, keep your dignity.

Akiko Taylor

REMEMBRANCE DAY

Annual salutations
Re-open old wounds,
Lacerating a valiant spirit.
Grief resurfaces,
A raging, tormented beast.
Its grotesque reincarnation
Casting dark shadows.
Repulsion spews
From every pore,
Drenching courage
With frailty
And weakness.
Commemorations thrust their swords
Deeper.
As fear feasts greedily
Like maggots on open flesh.

Valerie Caine

PRAYER TANK

Sunbeam watching, sundial slow, within a weekday church
Where two or three have gathered God is here.
From harvest time to Advent our Creator and our Judge
Our King, our Prince and Spirit welcome prayer.
International developments have brought us to our knees
According to His promises He hears our puzzled pleas
As the experts are deliberating far across the seas
Like St Peter we are trusted with the North Door keys.

By taking thought, we cannot reach conclusions
The world is full of clamour and despair
All we can do is bring Him our confusions
And trust that at each bedside He'll be there
The crisis internationally deepens with each hour
In the stained glass Eastern window, Jesus holds the orb with power.

Christopher Payne

A PERSONAL THOUGHT ON 9/11

Thirty years before, on a date then unnoticed but
Today remembered for another reason,
The horsemen of the Apocalypse rode into Chile.
Dictatorship replaced a democratically elected government.
Its leader shot - murder, arrest, torture and disappearance
Became the daily routine
For those who disagreed with the new regime.
How many now remember?

Which country released this pestilence on one whose
Philosophy of life contrasted with its own?
The very same which now expects the world
Not to forget that same date when horsemen came;
The day when the Twin Towers, symbols of American might,
                                        were destroyed
As if two teeth had been extracted from a smiling New York skyline.
Loved ones, never to return, were sought by grieving families
Experiencing the same emotions as others had thirty years before.

The sins of the forefathers
Are visited on the children
The Bible says.
But who remembers that today?

Peter French

SEPTEMBER 11TH 2001

In blue and silver and orange/black
Death came. Cruelly, and so considered.
An almost celluloid boomerang
Came back.
A cold precision. And,
Our world became not the same on that day,
(In our time)
Forever.

S Bonney

ACTS. LIKE 9-11

In compare
        Is love and warfare

And vengeful wrath
        Shall come to pass

But blind in action
        Is our great distraction.

Stuart Waldron

THE LIVING DEAD 9-11-01

Once he was chivalrous and tender
Only spoke words of affection,
Now he's contentious and rude,
His unending patience all but gone.
There were times when we would converse
For hours whilst dining with friends,
Not anymore, his tolerance diminished
Cherished memories are all I have left.
'Lucky to be alive,' they said,
With so many dead.

Would never believe that trivial things
Like doing the washing,
Would become such an issue
The shrill pitch of the spin
Echoes of the plane coming in!
The noise of children playing
Reminiscent of the chaotic confusion.
Still, 'Lucky to be alive,' they said,
With so many dead.

He's not the man I married
The fault not of his making,
He has no control of his actions
Whilst I, no control of my life.
So as you pay tribute, as time goes on
To all those lives lost, that fateful day
Spare a thought for those who were witness
The lucky survivors of that atrocity
Who have become the living dead!

Annette Murphy

NEON

When dulled down, shock painfully became
a pickaxe behind shimmering eyes,
the bludgeoning screen hammered memory cells
repeatedly, over and over.
Tears exploded, soft rain dampened flame,
the grumbling dust cloud debris disguised
broken hearts bursting in agonised swells
        searching for life confirmation.

Crashed vultures, evil in senseless flight,
beating humanity for hours like a drum,
cramping the breath with holocaust claws,
gleefully gloating, gloating.
Yet humanity does not die in the night,
by the warped wicked ways of fanatical scum,
humanity fades not, nor crawls on all fours
        the prey of abomination.

Could Hitler pulverise humanity dead?
Could Stalin annihilate its very soul?
Could Hussein defile its essence to dust?
Could they, Hell!
It arises from rubble and ashes instead,
steel resurrection, reassembled whole,
in the love and pride of people it must
        elicit restoration.

Beneath the veil of despair-crippled night
a broken city seethed neon till morning,
mortal wounds blazed and shone in rebirth,
defiantly living, living.
And hope prevailed in each bulb burning bright,
in each filament, tube, each spark a new dawning
of all that Heaven allows on Earth,
        a prayer-shot inspiration.

The carnage of angels bedazzled with pain,
yet the courage and conscience of saints empowered
a neon-lit love of brother for brother,
a blinding, blinding sight.
From sorrow and sacrilege raining again
humanity's wonder, upon them was showered
the love of the brave and the just for each other
        that they become the light.

Tony Bush

9-11

The world will never be allowed
To e'er forget that day
When numerous thousand families mourned,
. . . If media have their way.

Because it was *America,*
That 'powerful' 'greatest land',
The place where wealth and riches
Are as tiny grains of sand.

But what about poor Bali,
Israel, Palestine,
Or even Northern Ireland
And others down that line?

They're not remembered year 'pon year,
Is their grief not the same?
Of those, by buying bombs and guns,
America helped to maim?

Oh yes, 'twas an atrocity,
But then, 'Life *must* go on'
And let us live it to the full,
Enjoying each chronon.

Let families mourn in privacy,
As likely, all year through
They miss and grieve their lost and loved
Like most of us would do.

Colin Ross

SCHIPOL TO HEATHROW 9/11

It was an old world, Amsterdam
Older than we knew,
Its gabled houses, gliding canals
Lingered in our sunshine memories.
Its cobbles echoed through a seamless history
Greatness, decline and horrors intermingling
With our carefree present.

Boarding the plane, only the crew
Knew. They had heard the news
Seen the blanketing smoke, the raging fires.
The crashing planes screamed
Behind their eyes as they boarded.
The passengers, preoccupied,
Cocooned in trains and taxis
Still lived in unknowing bliss.

Only the crew knew; bravely boarded
Supervised, demonstrated, smiled.
We did not understand or register
The veiled assurances about security.
We read, they served, we ate, we chatted
Having no thought, no inkling
We should savour the passing of our world.

Innocent, we stole another hour
Sheltered by ignorance.
London unfolded safely below.
The pasted smiles dismissed us.
Luggage-laden we exited
Our airport chrysalis
And found we were new-born,
Blind in a terror-frosted world.

Sylvia Goodman

FLYING ON THE 11TH SEPTEMBER

I also flew on the 11th September,
Of course my thoughts reflect and remember,
With the Bone Marrow Trust,
I went to Slovenia,
For a sponsored walk,
In the month of September,
We raised much funds,
Helping others,
Less fortunates,
Our sisters and brothers,
Helping them build,
Their lives once more,
Please help their cause,
We all implore,
Those images
Will always stay,
Forever in our minds,
Twin Towers they imploded,
Shocking all mankind.

W Curran

New York's Finest

St Patrick's Day, did you parade,
And give your dollars to Noriade?
A token tithe from your pay,
Earmarked for the IRA?

And yet not think that others might
Also believe they had the right,
To kill and maim
In 'Freedom's' name?

And you, a hero, of those hours,
Amidst the havoc of the towers,
Don't see the difference is a name,
The provos, Al'Queda, just the same.

Christopher Pearce

PAVANE

With military precision dance the days,
pace by tear-stained pace stepping down the years.
No free-form gleeful thrash of flowing limbs,
this is a stately formal putting down of feet,
a 'show-no-feelings' mask to hide the pain.
Tomorrow - no! Tomorrow must not see
the hurt the world can't share but thinks it owns.
Only through the dance can day blur into day
and grief become a garment patched and torn
and patched until the tears become the cloth.
No privacy allowed: hold your head high
and meet the world's gaze between the eyes
defying with decorum those who seek to pry.
Two years or ten - the price is paid each day
by kith and kin of those who gave their all
in martyrdom's pavane - on both sides.

Lynn M Cochrane

PRIME AGENDA

(Dedicated to those who lost their lives in the Twin Towers tragedy)
(A *Millenielle Sonnet*)

When man reveals his darker hand
He turns God's spectrum black and white,
Then twisted shadows replace light
To guide him through this chosen land.

When devout minds bypass that link,
Which joins with ever-knowing heart,
They sever love and faith apart -
Then *'We Are Right'* is all they think.

But without love what future can
Be found where faith has risen cold?
Sunrise or sunset yet untold
Now greets this lost and regressed man.

*Seek the light, with faith that's tender
and make love the 'Prime Agenda'!*

Ian Deal

LIFE IS FOR LIVING

Taste death, because it's on the menu
And there's not a damn thing that you can do
So acquire the taste then with diligence
Let go of your fears and false pretence
That it'll never happen to you
We all expire, when our time is through

We need to be aware, that today is no rehearsal
However you have spent it, there can be no reversal
Comes tomorrow, today becomes yesterday
Whatever you did, will never again pass your way

Life is for living, on a positive tip
So enjoy every moment, while you're still on the trip
If humans were devoid of mortality
Then in our world there would be, no history

Ainsley McKenzie

I'M A BAD PERSON

All the animals I never felt guilty of eating,
All the truths I never believed,
All the abuses I knew about and never reported,
All the words I inflicted on others.

All the times I never cared,
All the angry words I yelled,
All the silent treatment I responded with,
All the things I said and never did.

All the vengeful punishments I dealt out,
All the bitter feelings I felt,
All the people I let down,
In all the situations I never helped out.

All the items I stole from shops and friends,
the list goes on and on, it never ends,
cause I'm a bad person, I'm nothing special,
but you wouldn't know unless I told you about them.

Heidi Dungate

FOX-HUNT

Run! Run!
They're on your tail
Don't dare look back!

They scent your trail!

And your heart
is pounding inside your fear
As you sense their frenzy

drawing near

They come at you out of the woods
- a bugle call - and horses' hooves

      You can't outrun
their brutal chase

. . . Such a high
           price to pay . . .
for fighting hunger every day

And now you've nearly run your race
         hopeless dizziness
choking your breath

And stumbling over
a fallen log

They're on you like
         a pack of dogs

Lifting you high to the baying crowd
of laughter in bright
jackets red

And thrown among the rabid throats -

Your last thought of your
child so cold

     . . . So alone now in her dread

As the slavering jaws rip
your soul to shreds

Steve Gunning

THE BIG ISSUE # 2

This ain't no story 'bout Jackanory
Or the cow that jumped over the moon
It's about people you meet on Heartbreak Street
There's no guarantee you won't be there soon

Now I know you spit phlegm when you condemn
But what's to say it won't happen to you?
Sure there are cases where men wear false faces
But in all walks of life this is true

I'll tell you a song, it won't take very long
You can sing the whole thing in a whisper
I met a young girl who set my mind in a whirl
I knew I loved her the first time I kissed her

There was no excuse for her whiskey abuse
From sweetness to sour took her no time
But the thing that I did when she killed our kid
Really had no reason or rhyme

Repentance didn't fill her, I took a gun to kill her
And the jury showed some compassion
I was not on the loose, though I begged for the noose
I got out early as was the law's fashion

My life was a pale and when I left jail
'Twas the first time that I had no home
I wasn't drugless, due to folks' smugness
In their safe houses of plastic and chrome

So now I've been cured and you're getting bored
On your doorstep you won't want me landing
But I still feel the bile when I think of the child
And see some of the crap from where I am standing

There's a moral or course, don't spend it all on one horse
You can have this advice, no, it's for free
Take away that false smile, you ain't seen your next mile
It could easily be you, 'stead of me!

E A Gifford

No, Leave The Lights On

spontaneous interjection
of smouldering, be-stilled passion
in Cosmic translucent completion
as our auras collide intermingled
'no, leave the lights on'
to savour our eyes meeting

instantaneous encapsulation
of Karmic bestowed desires
panoramic intoxication on cue
serenity of vision, of you
'no, leave the lights on'
and absorb fluttering hearts beating

oceanic tidal seduction
of climatic sought collision
endless endeavour answered
in momentary erotic collusion
'no, leave the lights on'
enjoy soft, moist, warm intrusion

exploratory empathic placement
in soft genital caresses
absorbed in the spasmodic nectar
of sublime harmonious contortion
'no, leave the lights on'
like to see who - I'm eating

breathtakingly stupendous
orgasmic elevation
in copulating cataclysmic union
enthralling totality of oneness
'no, leave the lights on'
as I watch your limbs undulating

sobriety of intention
culmination of anticipation
all embracing entirety of
catapulting ejaculations
'no, leave the lights on'
to savour the moment - redo each other
again, again, again, again . . .

Gary J Finlay

I'M FEELING WRECKED UP ON THE FLOOR

Don't take this ganja this off a me
I can't smoke it anymore
My eyes are shut I just can't see
I'm feeling wrecked up on the floor

I'm feeling wrecked up on the floor
I'm feeling wrecked up on the floor
I'm feeling wrecked up on the floor
I'm feeling wrecked up on the floor

The munchies I hear. I feel that sound
I can't fight them anymore
The dark paranoia's coming down
I'm feeling wrecked up on the floor

I'm feeling wrecked up on the floor
I'm feeling wrecked up on the floor
I'm feeling wrecked up on the floor
I'm feeling wrecked up on the floor

John Lee

HAM-FISTED

'Ham-fisted, ham-fisted,
ham-fisted, ham-fisted'
Oh the cries that I heard, they were only matched
by the 'Why?' the 'Why?' in my head
'He's ham-fisted, he's ham-fisted
brains too short, they stop at his wrists
he's ham-fisted, he's ham-fisted
watch his fingers as they struggle and twist'
I tried to explain it's not for lack of trying
I know I'm clumsy, yeh, there's no denying
but it's not my fault, nature played a trick
it isn't fair I should get so much stick
the doctor says there's a medical cause
responsible for my physical flaws
he says that nature will compensate
but I could only reply, that when it does
it'll probably be too late
'cause I'm worried sick the name's gonna stick
gonna leave me bitter and twisted
'Ham-fisted, ham-fisted'

John Coughlan

STRONG WORDS

The strongest words I know
Are not profane expletives,
But words that lift the heart
And keep one's spirits up -
Words like whole, perfect, strong,
Powerful, loving, harmonious and happy . . .
Words that assure me
That I am master of my fate
Through the quality of my thoughts!

Dan Pugh

THE HAPPY PILL MAN

Excuse me everybody would you like to gather round
I will speak to one or two of you but I would rather have a crowd
I would like to tell of the places that I love to go
I'm in you every clubbing night I know you love me so

I am the happy pill man, that guy you love to meet
Just not in front of everyone I live up that secret street
You boil me, you snort me, sometimes put me in a fag
You swallow me with Lucozade my existence how so sad

Then off into that thing I go you swirl me around
You wait for me to disappear then you listen to that sound
You listen to that progressive beat you listen to that trance
I start to make you feel real good you go off up there to dance

Off you go into that bubble you pound the night away
No need for conversation not much for you to say
I make you feel so happy man everybody is your friend
You kiss and give them cuddles you will love them to the end

Then off into the night I go I start to drift away
You float to Noddy Land and back I'm sadly on my way
Next week we will meet again of that I'm sure about
I can't wait to give you rushes see you dance and float about

The Unknown Poet

SHOOT THE BASTARDS

Seagulls, how I love them
Each and every one
Plucked and stuffed and mounted
Now wouldn't that be fun?

Shoot the bastards
Shoot the bastards
Bang, bang, bang
First I'll get the leader
Then I'll get his gang

I'd like to hang out the washing
As the weather is nice and fine
But then I decide not to, why?
The bastards are sitting on my line

Get the bastards
Get the bastards
Bang, bang, bang
First I'll get the leader
Then I'll get his gang

I'll make them a great big buttie
Cos it's the kind of girl I am
I'll fill it full of chilli
With just a touch of jam

Feed the bastards
Feed the bastards
I don't give a hang
First I'll get the leader
Then I'll get his gang

Poorly bastards
Poorly bastards
Of course, I'll do all I can
First to get the leader
Then to get his gang

Now I'm not an unkind person
I wouldn't hurt a fly
Yet when I see a seagull
I just want it to die

Bye, bye bastards
Bye, bye bastards
Never to return?
Oh no, there's a pigeon!
Will they never learn?

Sally-Ann Hayes

BEDTIME PRAYER

Midnight
no holes to run into
except sleep
when and if it comes
full of disturbance

Paedophile gangs grabbing
playing children from me
and ex-girlfriends
wearing collars of cum
have been this week's
dream-time cast

I've just finished my bottle
and there's no more
so I'm gonna finish this
by saying I hope
my morning coffee
tastes good - night.

Bryan Lynch

MENTALLY SCARRED

I would say unsociable neighbours
        and road rage drivers with their cars
Must have a mental failing
        with actions so bizarre

To do such things is childish
        and not from a developed brain
When they try to harm a neighbour
        it is caused through mental strain

Those people can't enjoy this life
        unless they are depraved
For friendship is the finest thing
        which at no time should be waived

To plague and annoy your neighbour
        who has not done you any harm
Then it's time to see a psychiatrist
        when your brain cells ring out their alarm

Lachlan Taylor

FEAR OF KNIVES

As the knife comes towards me,
As it touches my skin
I back away, but it cuts right in,
A deep wound down my chest
My last words are spoken
Before I go into a deep rest.
The knife is still in me;
All this feels like a memory,
I feel my neck begin to crack,
My bones are broken
In my arms and back.
The blood is enough to fill the sea,
The wound is deeper than deeper can be.
A slit across my wrists,
A slash across my throat,
Buried with the weapon
In my own coat.
So now can you see why I'm full of fear
Whenever a knife comes really near?
Why I shiver and I want to cry?
Why I feel like I'm going to die?
Don't think that I could cope,
If I ran out of life as well as hope,
Can't you see why I hate knives?
The thought of blood, murder and gore?
Because it feels to me;
Like I've already been killed by one,
Stabbed, slashed and wounded
In a real life nightmare,
Sometime, somewhere before.

Emma Louise Ashley

NOT ON MOUNT RUSHMORE BUT ON A SPIKE ON TRAITORS' GATE

Sacrificed: our control of territorial boundary by Blair giving up veto -
Another promise broken of 2001 Election manifesto.
Making government impotent in control of number of asylum seekers,
And further lining the pockets of corrupt lawyers.
He should go, for by his action he has shown himself to be unfit to
Govern this nation,
Unfitness already shown when he made Ms Morris - The Secretary for
Skills and Education.

R Wiltshire

SPREE

Went in every pub
In the small
Market town:
Called into the Bay Horse
Three times;
Landlord looked confused
Or could it have been me?

Alan Holdsworth

A LIGHT IN THE DARK

I've been around for a good many years,
And I just don't have a care,
I have one striking feature,
Everyone loves my red hair,
You couldn't call me lazy,
Because I was keen to work,
I never liked the blustery wind,
In odd little places, it would sometimes lurk.
We may come in all shapes and sizes,
We are needed worldwide, I would say,
No matter how much you might pay,
I always work well and I'm always up to scratch,
I'm just your faithful servant,
I'm your ordinary household match.

James Ayrey

A QUESTION OF FAITH

You ask so much of me,
You who made miracles,
Created Judaism,
Hand clapping
And religious euphoria
Now translated into Holy War,
Governments
With unbelievable politicians,
Children murdered
All-night searches
Cloning,
Anti-abortion pills,
Drugs
And super-bugs
Suicide bombs
And crying churches,
Dear God,
I need more than the Holy Ghost.

Could you send me a current photograph
And be my pen friend?
Is all that you created
About to end?
Computers
And futuristic shrouds,
And me praying out loud,
Amo, Amas, Amat . . .

Margarette Phillips

BLACK THOUGHTS

The horror of finding you're a fraud,
Has left my life strangely flawed,
For the meanwhile,
I must go into exile.

Those who weave nasty spells,
Will burn in their own hells,
Pretending to raise demons by horrid incantations,
You may well be trapped within your own frustrations,
You may stir up more than you can handle,
Disagreeable things happen, ensued by scandal
You have turned to dealings from sharpish practice
Into sheer dishonesty and lies,
Is it the pressure of circumstances, the unsure response
Of an unhappy person who denies,
These accusations when confronted the next day?
Burning black, vengeful candles glittering away,

He's somehow trying to get inside your secret soul to find,
The key to control . . . your mind
Suffering from really horrid, murderous, obsessive thoughts,
He knows the dangers that in his own trap he could get caught,
Planning revenge in a morbid way,
As you try to leave - he's trying to make you stay.
Dabbling in black magic,
Can be dangerous and even tragic!

Sheena Qureshi

BABYLON HISTORY 1-999

The Millennium Parasite Bugs
Bite hard
The bloody bloodsuckers

Man-made havoc!
Need the dependant culture of
Technology
Dream the dreamer
To escape reality?
Live the real nightmare
Where the nightmare is really real

Any town
Any city
Any county
Any country, anywhere

North or south
Of the fat equator
Any time zone, anywhere

The glass Oracle
Forecast the future
The live News are in any house
Any mud hut anywhere
Telly addicts are
Anywhere and everywhere

Nuclear electric
Electric Blue, really blue
Nuclear waste? Nobody wants a
Nuclear toxic garbage dump,
Anywhere

Nuclear threat
Nuclear holocaust
Burn the nuclear heat of hate
The furnace of Hell

Kalashnikov! Kalashnikov!
Widow maker
Sing the gun, the requiems
Sing the singer
The rhapsody of bloody hell!

Babylon, Babylon
Recite, recite
Propaganda, the garbage of the lips
The sacrament of hate, is the last sacrament
Political dogma!
Political ideology!
Democracy? Dictatorship?
The slaves are always
Waiting to be bought and sold
Anywhere! Everywhere.

T Lawrence

BOREDOM CUBED

Rattle rattle
Spitter-spatter
The rain drilled the caravan roof
And trickled down the window
The wee boy sighed
It's like sitting in a tin can
Someone bring a tin opener
And let out the frustration
He sniffs the smells of breakfast
And hears the kettle whistling
Announcing afternoon tea
With Penguin biscuits
On holiday in a metal box
The raindrops chasing down the window
He wished he was anywhere but here
Seamill
Ayrshire
1970:

Ian Speirs

CANNIBAL KILLER

I sharpen my knife
On tears from your eyes.
I get my pleasure
From between your thighs.

To rape and to kill
Releases my pain,
Just like the knife
Cutting into your brain.

I love to kill.
Such a thrill
I get to watch you die.
I love to kill.
Such a thrill
To watch your blood run dry.

You look so sexy
All cut up and bled.
A dozen severed pieces
In a pool of crimson red.

Just looking at you
All cut up and dead,
Drives me into a frenzy
And gives me 'good head'!

I love to kill.
Such a thrill
To cut your flesh apart.
I love to kill.
Such a thrill
To cook and eat your heart.

Peter Steele

LET'S GIVE THANKS

Thank you Aristotle for letting me know
That I'm a failed man because my penis didn't grow.

Thank you Timothy for reminding me not to speak
I hold my tongue in silence for my mind is weak.

Thank you Jerome for encouraging me to slim
To mutilate and flagellate and starve away my sin.

Thank you Ambrose for encouraging virginity
For spurning sex in marriage and teaching me of chastity.

Thank you Augustine you taught me of concupiscence
That men fell through women and I am ever in subservience.

Thank you Tertullian I *am* the gateway of the Devil
Who broke the glass of God's great image, in that I must not revel.

Thank you Aquinas for reminding me I'm defective
That I'm misbegotten and from the world must be rejected.

Thank you Spenger for the *Malleus Maleficarum*
Warn the world what witches do and of course it's right to burn them.

For my duty to die in childbirth, thank you Martin Luther
Of course it does not matter for that is what I'm here for.

Thank you Dr Acton you taught me to be a little girl,
Sexless, modest and submitting to my husband's will.

Thank you Mr Ruskin, you placed me on a pedestal
An alabaster angel, enduring and infallible.

Christian love reaches women in so many thoughtful ways
Man has redeemed me in the eyes of God and for this I give him praise.

E D Darling

WHAT NEEDLES ME!

I know before I start this that I will be branded a racist pig,
But I don't want to back off and be branded as not caring a fig,
I'm a person who has always believed in charity starting at home,
with our own,
And all these pensioners and kids in poverty in my opinion come
into this zone.

Our Government allows terrorists in, supported by our state funding
and grants,
That's even after they have scared everybody out of their pants,
If we make comment the Civil Rights people are at our throats,
When they should be helping these folk back in aeroplanes and boats

I saw all these people during the war and after when serving abroad,
They didn't like the British Empire and all it stood for then, Good Lord,
But when you give them independence they make matters worse
than ever,
Then blame it on us, claiming that they are clever.

Education and discipline were applied in rightful measure,
We didn't burn down the farms and places providing the treasure,
Now many are in a state of famine and need,
Just because of their so-called 'elected leaders' greed.

So let us start by kicking out all these offensive yobs,
Who are recruiting terrorists for their next bombing jobs,
All this yammer about our record as Colonialists in the 1800s say,
Cannot be blamed on the people of this country today.

Jack Edwards

FIRE-FIGHTERS' STRIKE

No matter
What the reasons are
Or whoever are the liars
It seems that
Until we pee in your pot
You won't piss on our fires
It's easy sometimes
To feel hard done by
And Christ - yes
We've all been broke
But a child
Won't understand all this
If their world
Goes up in smoke.

Brian Thomas

BE COURAGEOUS

Boost your life like the breeze of the sea
Make the life easy for your best
Actually, the world is full of war
Challenges come in every second
Inside this storm of life
Fight slowly and win the battle
Either good or bad, directly or strategically
The world is not a thing to face alone
Slow and steady wins the race
Easy doing is the key to the world
Today may seem rough and full of sorrow
Make yourself a happy figure
Happy flower gives the best odour
Work of years may end in vain
Struggles of years may be falling consecutively
Insults from friends and relatives may worsen the condition.
Never lose hope, patient dog eats the fattest bone
Downfall of a person is never the end
Never think it has gone till final whistle is blown
Life goes on and the chances still continue
To be a hero is never a joke
You must be ready to climb from obscurity to greatness
History will never be sweet to tell without difficulty
Be courageous and have confidence
Any soul that is not confident is twice defeated in the race of life.
Any time, any day, be courageous
Even if your career programme is rough and tough
Or your record of performance is mere disappointment and failure
Still, let the struggle continue
Because only those who fight and conquer wear the golden crown.

Ojo Idowu Opeyemi

So Glad I'm Not At Oxford

So glad I'm not at Oxford
Because I'm one of those
Who has much less to offer them.
Correct? We'll see. Who knows!

Scandal - overcoming loss
Means I'm not up to scratch
The deaf don't get the picture whole
But only snitch and snatch.

Lip-reading sometimes let us down
Your signing can be poor
Try 'reading' from the 'non-aware'
Who gesture, shout and roar!

Other applicants, you said
Were in much finer fetter
But remember, dons, my grades were gained
By harder work and better!

Communicator at my side
Ensures equality.
Why can't I, as my hearing peers,
Enter university?

For despite my lifelong struggle
To achieve my full potential
It's hearing folk who lack some sense
Where extra work's essential.

One sense less makes sharper four
We never miss a sign
You with sound have far to go
To cross fine line of mine.

Di Castle

ALEX'S WORLD

Fill me up with the jungle juice,
My life is such a mess,
I can't take it anymore,
I'm sick of all the stress.

I don't go to church,
Cos church is full of old gits.
I don't give to charity,
Cos charity's full of twits.

I don't go to work,
Cos working tires me out,
And this flipping government
Makes me wanna shout.

Lorraine Green

MUM AND SON

'Ta-ta Mum, I'm off out now,' said the teenage man in half a shout.
'Well comb your hair and brush your teeth and don't come home
too late,
Unless of course you are going on another extended date,
Don't go without your little cover, you know what I mean
And in case you have an accident, make sure your pants are clean,
If she is the sort of girl I would like you to see,
Bring her home here and she can stay for tea,
Later on you might go to bed and have a little poke,
But if you put her up the duff that will be no joke,
If you ignore my words and play the fool,
You will pay for that child, until the child leaves school
And if I were her instead of me,
That child would not leave school until aged thirty-three!'

Roy Kimpton

START TO FINISH

So you told me all I know love just did grow
The seed did sow, flowers bloom much room
So you said you loved me, I was well in the Bell
Perhaps these lines may seal true love as well

The children came, tried to work give very best
Was for me no time for rest all skills had to test
Your words told me know in heart was red glow
Did turn brain and heart insane, eyes salt rain

You gave my all away became my darkest day
Now have we really nothing left, sorry little deaf
Keypad no secret in your heart, knew from the start
Only that I loved you, should other's played part

Not too late to little this can be said for everything
Let's make one promise please put hatred in bin
Please show world mountains far from too steep
Sorry about rubbish heap, love you but must sleep

Now must show world can take the madness it give
From start to finish why did our parents let us live
But you alone can kill me have known this from start
So if wish just finish before fate play its cruellest part

John J Flint

MR BLAIR

Dear Mr Blair, I'm in despair
For what you've done to me
Here I am sitting
By an old Iraqi tree.
I don't know these people
They've done nothing wrong to me:
Yet I've had to kill them
It's not right that I can see.
I thought we came to help them
I see now I was wrong
All that we have done
Is make them more strong.
You'll go down in history
With Maggie 'what's her name',
For she was good at sinking ships
Which brought about her fame.
As for John Major
Back to basics was his game
And after the Gulf war
Many men were not the same.
It's within our country the real fight is
A battle against drugs and crime
Yet you turn your head away
As if you haven't got the time.
This will come to haunt you
Now that is a crime,
For the Labour party you've destroyed
Which once was mine.

J Lanigan

WINSTON, WHERE ARE YOU NOW?

Tony is the man, that is supposed to lead,
yet tax payers money he seems to bleed.
Immigration is in crisis, the roads are in a mess,
but will this man in power, ever confess?
His manifest is nonsense, with front benchers thick as planks,
left wing leaning all the way, including all the banks.
The BBC's a mouthpiece, for all that labour cess,
They've taken the Great from Britain and left us in a mess.
They rubbish all our heritage and destroyed what made us great,
muggers walking on our streets, with faces filled with hate.
You can't get dental treatment, unless you have the dough,
and if you want good health care, then private you should go.
Its the same with education, going downhill with this mob,
jaded, tired teachers, not allowed to do their job.
With political correctness things have gone downhill,
where are you now we need you, Mr Winston Churchill?
Well, he just wouldn't take it, he'd have to make a stand,
he would fight them on the beaches, to save this fair land.
He'd stop the rot and stem the tide,
of pro Euro toadies who are on the rise.
He'd slam the door and bolt it tight,
saying, 'Brace yourself for a fight.'
He would turn the tide of bogus immigrants, who into this
                                            country glide,
he'd drop the Euro and stamp on crime,
making sure that killers and rapists served their time.
Oh boy, if only we could have him back,
we wouldn't have to put up with, a silly, grinning prat.

William H Hawkes

TONY BLAIR

Tony Blair
could hardly say he didn't care
about the world today
bombings, shootings, crime
his answer to go to war
few in numbers
war an evil from the past
America tall and strong super power
if there's one wrong thing today
it would be the war
but if there was one good thing
it would be the war
showing there is a force
willing to bring peace
men of steal values
man of stealth
heroes unsung
men intelligent no one could
ponder to understand
they have broken down some barriers
freed them
from the bomb carriers
gun carriers
peace
slaves are no more
women are free
thanks to brave men
at home jobs are taken away
shops are closing
commodities are fading
but this is England
let's cherish the food from our land
keep it so
freedom for all
what was wrong with cycles

weekends of rest
horses for transport
more people to do more
faster
pulling together without the greed
we have to
realise our precious minerals
are dwindled
but we can farm
and man needs warmth and food
the other gifts we have
precious but fading fast
new projects
solar power

Jennifer Dunkley

THE TENANTS LONG FIGHT

Six long years and here we are
Standing on the edge
Tony, Gordon and John Prescott
Driving in the wedge

Selling off the housing stock
Coal mines, railways gone
Now we tenants stand alone
Cos we're left, the only one

The backbone of the country
Communities at large
Giving homes to landlords
At very little charge

Has it been now six long years?
We hear the tenants wail
You go tell John Prescott
Our homes are not for sale.

Thomas M Glynn

TONY'S IN A SPIN

How do you climb the slippery pole
And somehow still manage to hang onto your soul?
Holding on grimly to the uttermost top
Try not to look down at the dizzying drop

After a few years you perfect a spin
To stop other climbers from thinking they'll win
Spinning and grinning and wonderfully winning
Or cheating and lying and sincerely sinning?

Tony the phoney is stuck up a pole
Not much different to stuck down a hole
Except high up we can see him cling on in despair
I think he's forgotten why he first climbed up there!

Eric Ferris

AS AT BLAIR WE STARE

Is he good or bad?
The lad. In Westminster
Sounds good not bad
The lad. Promising reformity

Not good very bad
Lords, hunt debacle
Asylum education muddle
Spin stealth NHS deformity

Can good be so bad?
On world stage at home rage
No good really bad
War war Iraqi intensity

Can good outdo bad?
Think. In Westminster
Bad is 'wait and see'
Much enormity in obscurity

Blair belief dogma
Rhetoric, queried trust
Rich poor all pay more
Man! Advocating equality

P A Findlay

DOUBLE TALK

Mr Blair, Mr Blair,
Making speeches everywhere,
Laughing off each niggling slur.
Ever keen to play things down.

Mr Blair, Mr Blair,
Pretending that you're playing fair,
Yet swift to grab the lion's share,
Of any credit or renown.

Mr Blair, Mrs Blair,
What a most delightful pair.
Hungry for the media's glare,
Never seen without a frown.

Mr Blair, Mr Blair,
Duping others when you dare,
Clouding issues so they blur,
Quoting stats until we drown.

Mr Blair, Mr Blair,
Creating 'fiction' here and there,
Embracing Bush without a care,
Playing war games like a clown.

Mr Blair, Mr Blair,
Secreted in your cocooned lair.
Are you making plans somewhere,
To be fitted for a crown?

Paul Kelly

IT'S MY WAR - AND I'LL LIE IF I WANT TO!

(Ode to a dodgy Prime Minister)

His second dossier was 'dodgy'
A fraud . . . ! It weighed a ton!
Designed to cheat democracy
And bounce us - everyone! -
Into a war for no just cause
When all is said and done . . .

That most of it was plagiarized
A candle-burning trawl . . .
'Downloaded' off the Net - *and out of date!* -
Is now quite plain to all
No 'current' view from JIC
'Intelligence' . . . ? - F**k all . . . !

The first, a few months earlier -
But just as false, I swear -
Gave undue prominence to threats
Hans Blix believed weren't there
And made too much of menaces
'Sexed-up' by Tony Blair

With 'spin' like this to hoodwink us
Blair strove to foment war
As Robin Cook, then Claire Short too
Agreed above the floor . . .
'A Campbell's soup of lies!' Cook sighed,
'W-well . . . 'Horlicks' . . . ?' gulped Jack Straw.

Whatever, there's now little doubt
Misinformation reigned
With unspun 'truth' and free debate
In Parliament constrained . . .
Blair's aims to bomb Iraq decided
But by subterfuge maintained

Not Bush, nor Blair, dared brook delay
Impatient - as one man! -
To crush dissent and spread alarm
With shit tossed at the fan . . .
Before an empty-handed UN search
Could thwart their battle plan

Meanwhile . . .
Invasion forces, sent in haste
To cheat the starter's gun
Deployed in depth around the Gulf
Declared the deed begun . . .
100,000 men - *and more!* -
'Blair's War' already 'won' . . . !

Joanna Jay

RICTUS

He came in grinning, or was it a leer?
PC to the core, though the women are bad enough
the men are worse, minds
mimicking a spatial black hole
sucking in any surrounding light
permitting nothing - nothing to escape.
No more may we gaze upwards
but must slouch, shuffling in our ranks,
hand on the shoulder of him, no, her
I mean the *person* in front
the blind, the deaf and the dumb.
Mother once said, 'As long as you have a tongue
you will never be lost - just ask the way.'
Ah, but what if the tongue must be still
for fear of being slit?
Poor dear, she fought with her idea of justice
against an evil she could see and understand,
but those hiding behind the curtain
contrive to bend us to their will, enforcing
a twisted idea, not native justice.
They prey on the blind, the deaf and the dumb,
who are treading on a path
winding to an horizon where the sky
smokes red, towards the terror of their inevitable end.

Richard Unwin

BLAIR WARE

Politicians are dyed in lies and truth
Action begets glory disdain
Inaction begins a tired refrain

Belief can turn into grief
Within a moments notice
There is no relief

Care for country or policy
Does not bode well
The balance as prime minister
Makes one pass or fail

James Patrick Milton

BROKEN PROMISES

They never kept their promises
and now the country's in despair
the scandal over Dr Kelly
will be the end of Blair

His government's in turmoil
it's a great big fairground ride
with the Tories on the waltzer
and Labour on the slide

Blair had dealings with a conman
many, think he lied about Iraq
playing roulette with the voters
has left him open to attack

With their failure to deliver
the public feel that they've been conned
it's just taxes, taxes, taxes
time for Labour to abscond

With the NHS collapsing
and all our pensions in the air
law and order out the window
they just don't seem to care

They are acting like dictators
they will not listen or take note
and on the issue over Europe
they have refused to let us vote

Asylum seekers still arriving
the situation's out of hand
the black labour market's thriving
as they spread throughout the land

Organised by pimps and bandits
these gangsters know the score
they see the UK as their oyster
and they treat is as their whore

Labour had their opportunities
but they've gone and blown the lot
and come the next election
they'll know we've not forgot!

T Britton

THE PRIVILEGED AND FORGOTTEN
(Upon the birth of Leo)

A privileged child is born,
While sanctions cause Iraqi children to die,
The PM sells photographs for charity,
His spin doctors nearby.
In New Labour's classless society,
A three-year-old boy is turned away,
Cancer is the problem,
The NHS can't afford to pay.

And in this week of news,
They throw more lottery money to the dome,
Deny Dunkirk's heroic craft,
Vital repairs and a home.

The PM takes paternity leave,
No minimum wage earner can afford,
But the PMs sickly smile never fades,
When our *saviour* is outdoors,
So forget the world's horrors,
Injustice, famine and wars,
Tony is a dad again,
Even doing fatherly chores.

Norman Dickson

VOTE FOR ME

Our love and freedom, peace and justice for all
False promises, but it's what they all say
And we'll lower taxes for the working Joe
Vote for me and it'll be here one day

But once they've got their seat
In the office behind the big desk
All the promises are dead meat
Just get fed, the scraps that are left

Not one of them gives us what we want
They all tell us what we want to hear
Not one is prepared to admit, it was all a sham
'Cause then they know it means defeat

Do they give us peace, love or freedom?
If you ask them what do they have to say?
And where's the justice or the lower taxes
You voted for me, just shut up and pay!

David McDonald

GROWING AWARE

This verse was written, through a stage in my life,
A mid-life crisis, as described by my wife.
It's not quite the crisis, as you may think,
So don't be nervous and head for the drink.
It's more about answers, to questions of life,
The sort you don't ask, so you don't scare the wife.
Why go on living, they won't miss me?
They're always so boring, just watching TV.
They won't go anywhere, just laze about
And when you say things, you all scream and shout.
You're working for nothing, you wish to be dead,
Then you feel daft, for the thoughts in your head.
The passion of love, no longer feels there
And what's even worse, you think she doesn't care.
The kids don't respect you; it's only your money,
Your humour seems old; you're no longer funny.
You lie in bed and plan the next day,
This one's the one, you can break away.
You know you can't do it, you wonder why,
Is there some force holding, that comes from the sky?
You question belief and thoughts in your mind,
Searching for answers, you think you can't find.
Think not of the future, nor dwell on the past,
Each day is passing, you must make it last.
Your marriage is worth, more than a fling,
So don't be tempted, by some little thing.
Go find a hobby, or something to do,
Whatever you're thinking, your wife will love you.
Trust in her love and what you once had,
Explain that you're lonely and feeling sad.
And if she's the woman, that once was your wife,
She'll promise to be there, for all of her life.

Sid 'de' Knees

2011

2011, ten years on
New World Trade Centre, ten storeys taller
Than the one those two planes blew up
Afghanistan obliterated, Osama Bin Laden blown to Hell

G W Bush attacked Bin Laden troops
With all the firepower of the US of A
The victor born on American soil
Sunday 11th September is VOBL Day

Graygrey and Debs at a victory street party
Rejoice and drink the night away
Making magic against the lamp post
Peace at last has come our way

H G Griffiths

STORY POEM

He was the new Archdeacon,
She was the vicar's wife.
He, tall, dark and handsome
Was about to change her life.
He came to see the parish,
The fabric of the church,
The wardens and congregation:
An ecclesiastic search.
On many a friendly visit
To pop in and jumble sale,
His careless, accidental touch
Made her feel weak and pale.
The unsuspecting vicar
Was flattered by the attention
And welcomed his friend, the Archdeacon,
Not sensing the burgeoning tension.
Summer days turned to autumn,
Then winter into spring;
She saw the time approaching,
The start of a secret fling;
Then horror on mounting horror,
As she waited for the word to be said -
The handsome, wicked Archdeacon
Chose his friend, the vicar, instead!

Ann Dodson

ELECTED

Let the people see you,
Make sure you are heard,
Put forward your viewpoint,
In understanding word.
Of course, you'll get disagreement,
Just keep a cool head,
Make sure you believe
Everything you said.
They are now beginning
To follow where you lead,
The picture becomes clearer,
With every line you read.
Soon the vote is taken,
Has your speech sunk in?
Yes, the vote is counted,
You've got a clear win.

E M Gough

THE TRUST HAS GONE

You came into power and the country was glad,
For we saw a man who knew good from bad.
Education, education, education, you cried,
Along with social justice and a reduction in crime.

But then came the spin and the gobbledegook,
An alliance with America and a Texan crook.
America, America, let us be friends,
You have such power and money to spend.

Where are the weapons that threaten us all?
Surely you know you sell them on call.
The soldiers you sent to join with the Yanks,
Who is most happy the arms dealers or banks?

We can't find bin Laden so what shall we do?
We know where Saddam is so he'll have to do.
Iraq is the new threat and so we must act,
We can't go alone, we must form a pact.

What happened to us at this time of alliance?
Did you forget while taking this stance?
The firefighter, the nurse, the teacher as well,
Public servants they are you can't seem to tell.

Why bother to vote now you all may wonder?
Does it really matter if I make a blunder?
Labour or Tory, Liberal or Green,
It makes little difference or so it would seem.

So where are we now, better or worse?
Are we any safer or have we a curse?
The country was pleased but now it is scared,
What happens next we don't know and we thought you cared?

Phil Peartree

EMPEROR'S NEW CLOTHES

It has come to my notice that the Blair government has decided to
                              abolish the General Election!
They do not consider the average voter has the intelligence to decide
                              who should govern this country!
Tony Blair will make the decision for them!

I am joking, don't worry!

But denying us a referendum on European Constitution implies
                              the above.

Surely we should have the final say once all the negotiations have
                              been made?

If we are denied this, the implication would be Tony has something
                              to hide.

In 1975 Harold Wilson cleverly offered the country its first referendum.
This was a ploy to silence the critics within his cabinet.

The outcome was a forgone conclusion, but in the process of open
Debate, the public became better informed.

Why does our Prime Minister shy away from this opportunity?

Is he afraid the electorate will discover he is only wearing a *fig leaf?*

Ben Wolfe

POWER OF THE MOON

My silent, sombre mood
Echoed in the murky twilight
As an ebony night
Like a stalking black shadow
Will soon engulf my very being
My wretched soul cries out
Begging that the silver demon
Will not show itself
From behind lurking clouds

I fear the power of the moon
I pleaded insanity
Thinking I would be safe
Locked away in deep shadows
But no, it's magnetic pull
Still reaches my very soul
I hear the night wind calling
Laughing, mocking me
With masochistic pleasure

I squirm in the darkness
From the window high above
The first rays of silvery light
Creep across the floor towards me
Vengeance will be mine tonight
When they least expect it
I will no longer be at their mercy
For my restless heart will find peace
And my troubled mind will be free

The pounding in my head
And fear in my eyes will be gone
They will curse me to my grave
But it will be too late
The moon cannot follow me

Beneath the cold, dark earth
The moonlight glints on the blade
Then my blood flows slowly
Across the floor to meet
The pool of moonlight.

Marisa Greenaway

CHARLES KENNEDY

The press, they grovel to Tony Blair,
But like his party, they're never there.
Tories, they made this country a mess,
So we can't trust that crazy IDS.
The only one the press don't see,
Is the hard work done by Charles Kennedy.
I think it's a conspiracy, something sinister,
That they don't show Charles, the Prime Minister.

He has the thing for every voter,
Be you new or finding your quota.
For half a century the same old story,
Boring Labour and stale, old Tory.
No wonder folk like any election,
What choice have you got from that selection.
There is someone, take it from me,
Vote Lib-Dem, elect Charles Kennedy.

Colin Allsop